Regal

PUBLISHED BY REGAL BOOKS
FROM GOSPEL LIGHT
VENTURA, CALIFORNIA, U.S.A.
PRINTED IN THE U.S.A.

Books is a ministry of Gospel Light, a Christian publisher dedicated
ving the local church. We believe God's vision for Gospel Light is to
de church leaders with biblical, user-friendly materials that will help
evangelize, disciple and minister to children, youth and families.

ur prayer that this Regal book will help you discover biblical truth for
own life and help you meet the needs of others. May God richly bless

free catalog of resources from Regal Books/Gospel Light, please call your
ian supplier or contact us at 1-800-4-GOSPEL or www.regalbooks.com.

s for publishing this book in other languages are contracted by
el Light Worldwide, the international nonprofit ministry of Gospel
. Gospel Light Worldwide also provides publishing and technical
ance to international publishers dedicated to producing Sunday
ol and Vacation Bible School curricula and books in the languages of
orld. For additional information, visit www.gospellightworldwide.org;
to Gospel Light Worldwide, P.O. Box 3875, Ventura, CA 93006; or
an e-mail to info@gospellightworldwide.org.

Moments Together

for

LIVING WHAT YOU B

Dennis and Barba Rainey

Regal

From Gospel Light
Ventura, California, U.S.A.

Re
to
pr
th

It
yc
yc

F
C

R
C
L
a
S
t
v
s

Cover and interior design by Rob Williams
Edited by Stephanie Parrish and Dave Boehi

Library of Congress Cataloging-in-Publication Data
Rainey, Dennis, 1948–
  Moments together for living what you believe / Dennis and Barbara
Rainey.
    p. cm.
  ISBN 0-8307-3348-5
  1. Meditations. 2. Christian life. I. Rainey, Barbara. II. Title.
  BV4832.3.R347 2004
  242—dc22   2003028054

1   2   3   4   5   6   7   8   9   /   09   08   07   06   05   04

INTRODUCTION

If you picked up this book, you probably desire to have loving relationships with God, your family and others. But if you're like us, you don't display that love consistently. Perhaps in prayer you've made a heartfelt commitment to the Lord to consistently show love to your spouse and children, but five minutes later you felt you were going to explode in anger.

You desire to obey God and follow His commandments, but sometimes you do the very thing you are trying to avoid. Why is that? The apostle Paul says it's because of our sinful nature, the "flesh" (Rom. 7:18). We have trouble living according to God's guidelines for having loving relationships because we have a will that is contrary to God's will.

Moments Together for Living What You Believe is for those who, like us, have trouble living out what they believe. Fortunately, God has given us direction in His Word, the Bible, on how to deal with this problem. In this devotional, which is based on God's Word, you'll find help and insight on topics such as fearing God, self-denial, commitment to marriage, and loving the unlovable. And you'll also see that God has provided a Helper for us to be able to resist the desires of our sinful nature and to live according to His will: the Holy Spirit. He is the only One who can give us the power to obey God.

Our prayer is that you will be challenged and encouraged as you work through the 30 days of this devotional. And always remember, it's impossible to live what we believe in our own power—we need to draw on the power God provides when we trust in Him.

HOW DO YOU VIEW GOD?

[Moses replied to Pharaoh,] "May it be according to your word, that you may know that there is no one like the LORD our God."

EXODUS 8:10

Where do we get our concepts of God? Of who He is and how He operates this world that He created and sovereignly rules over?

Kids give us glimpses of how we used to think or, for many of us, how we still think. I ran across a little book that contained letters from children to pastors. Here are some excerpts:

"Dear Pastor, I know God loves everybody, but he never met my sister."

"Dear Minister, I would like to bring my dog to church on Sunday. She is only a mutt, but she is a good Christian."

Here's one that speaks of our culture: "I would like to read the Bible, but I would read it more if they would put it on TV."

And finally: "Dear Pastor, I would like to go to heaven someday because I know my big brother will not be there."

A friend of mine in Denver overheard his daughters' conversation during a thunderstorm one day. The older daughter said matter-of-factly, "That thunder you just heard is God moving His furniture."

The younger daughter nodded her head like she understood and looked out the window at the pouring rain for a minute before she replied: "Yes, He just moved His waterbed, too."

Come on, admit it. You and I have some pretty silly notions about God, too. Some of us view Him as a giant policeman up in heaven with a club, while others see Him only as a loving grandfather figure.

But God is so much more than one or the other. He's infinite. He's sovereign. He is to be feared and worshiped and loved. Honestly, how do you view God?

Discuss: Make a list of adjectives or word pictures that describe your honest view of God.

Pray: Find a Bible concordance (the one in the back of your Bible will do). Look under "God" and read down through the verses, jotting down what God is and isn't. Take a moment to confess your misconceptions about Him, and worship Him using this new list.

GOD IS SO MUCH MORE
THAN A LOVING GRANDFATHER
FIGURE OR A GIANT
POLICEMAN UP IN HEAVEN.

NOTES ON BEING GOOD

Thanks be to God that . . . you became obedient from the heart to that form of teaching to which you were committed.

ROMANS 6:17

One day our son Samuel, then eight, typed out a treatise titled "How to Be Good." Here is his own unedited work, shared with his permission:

HOW TO BE GOOD

1. Obay you parntes and GOD.
2. Do want other kids want to do.
3. Do not be selfish.
4. Be good to babbysearts.
5. Do want parntes say.
6. Do not cheat.
7. Play right.
8. Be a good player.
9. Dont be a por sport.
10. Do no cuse.

Not bad, is it? Who knows what triggered this active boy to jot down this inspired list. Samuel's conclusions are a child's perception of several of the Ten Commandments. And he may know them a little better than most adults.

When I look at the Ten Commandments, I see that the first two alone are a good summary of how to be good.

The first commandment is "You shall have no other gods before Me" (Exod. 20:3). While Israel was tempted to worship idols, I'm convinced that one of modern Christianity's worst forms of idolatry is materialism. Barbara and I constantly evaluate this issue because we don't want to leave a legacy of materialism for our kids.

Another form of idolatry is our worship of self-fulfillment. Careers, the number of children we decide to have, our attitudes about divorce—all have been sired by the personal-rights movement.

The second commandment is "You shall not take the name of the LORD your God in vain" (v. 7). Taking God's name in vain is more than just using His name as a swear word. It is taking His name to mean nothing. Even the phrase "Praise the Lord" can lose its meaning when we say it only out of habit. God is holy and sacred, the God to be feared. Swearing is thoughtlessly speaking of Him in a non-God-fearing way.

We know that these commandments (along with the other eight) contain a moral snapshot of God's nature, holiness and goodness. Philosophers try to find out God's nature by reason. Believers discover who He is as they walk in obedience to His Word.

Discuss: Read and discuss the Ten Commandments from Exodus 20:1-17 at your next family meal.

Pray: Pray that doing God's will may become an inner urge in your heart, not just a dutiful observance of external commands.

FEARING GOD
(PART ONE)

I will give heed to the blameless way. When wilt Thou come to me? I will walk within my house in the integrity of my heart.

PSALM 101:2

Some boys were tempting a young lad to pull a prank with them. The three young men taunted the other lad, "Come on, do this with us. Nobody will find out."

Finally, the boy mentioned his father. So they taunted him further. They said, "Oh, you're just afraid because if your father finds out, he might hurt you!" And the boy looked back at the others and said, "No, I'm afraid if he finds out, it'll hurt him."

The fear of God is reverential awe and respect for Him. It is a heartfelt conviction that He is not only loving and personal but also holy and just. Bill Gothard says fearing God is "the conscious awareness that God is watching everything and evaluating everything I think, say and do." God sees all. He knows all. He's evaluating all.

The more you fear God—the more you spend time in His presence—the more you dread displeasing Him. His presence in our lives shouldn't be a heavy yoke around our necks. But we need to have a healthy dread of displeasing, hurting or disappointing Him.

If you could stand before God today in His throne room and watch a video of your life with Him, would there be a smile on His face? Would He be nodding His head in approval, saying, "Well done, thou good and faithful servant" (Matt. 25:21, *KJV*)? Would you like to have the confidence right now that God is smiling? You can—by beginning to respect Him, to practice the presence of God daily and to make your choices on the basis of what pleases Him.

At any point of time during the day, I would like to be ready to be ushered into the presence of God and see a smile of approval on His face. I don't want Christianity to be a spare tire, fire insurance or something that is just there to bail me out of trouble. I want to walk with Jesus Christ moment by moment, yielded to the power of the Holy Spirit.

The fear of the Lord, then, should be a powerful, motivating factor in our lives. We shouldn't be legalistic about it, viewing God with a giant flyswatter in the sky, ready to crush us when we displease Him.

Let this new concept of a healthy fear of God refresh you. Let the presence of God refurbish you. Practicing Christ's presence in your life will set you free.

Discuss: Do you have a regular sense of being in God's presence? What will practicing the presence of God in your life liberate you to do?

Pray: Ask God to make Himself real to you and to give you a divine sense that He is watching you and waiting to spend time with you.

IF YOU COULD STAND
BEFORE GOD IN HIS
THRONE ROOM AND WATCH
A VIDEO OF YOUR LIFE,
WOULD THERE BE A
SMILE ON HIS FACE?

FEARING GOD
(PART TWO)

*And they shall be My people, and I will be their God;
and I will give them one heart and one way, that they may
fear Me always, for their own good, and for the good of their
children after them. And I will make an everlasting
covenant with them that I will not turn away from them,
to do them good; and I will put the fear of Me in their
hearts so that they will not turn away from Me.*

JEREMIAH 32:38-40

Why do you think God wants us to fear Him? Perhaps because there are benefits to us for fearing Him.

Just look at the verses above. Here we see that God wants to do us good and promises He will not turn away from us. But He also does not want us to turn away from Him. Let's look at a few reasons why.

First, *the fear of God is the fountain of life for the believer.* Proverbs 22:4 says that the fear of God, along with humility, leads us to wealth, honor and life. And Psalm 111:10 says that the fear of God gives us skill in life and provides wisdom. A healthy respect, or fear, of God is the key to life.

Second, *the fear of God builds faithfulness in the believer*. This passage from Jeremiah tells me that the fear of God has been riveted into our souls by the Holy Spirit to keep us faithful. The true test of any man or woman is not what we do when everyone is looking. The real test is what we would do if we knew no one would find out.

Fearing God means we practice His presence in our lives daily—nothing is hidden from Him. He sees everything. He knows everything. We can't hide in the darkness and sin. We can't sneak away from His all-seeing eyes or omnipotent mind. And, yes, that does keep us faithful.

Third, *God fulfills the desires of those who fear Him*. Psalm 145:19 says, "He will fulfill the desire of those who fear Him; He will also hear their cry and will save them." Fearing God doesn't just keep us from sin; it leads us out of trouble.

May God etch the fear of Him on our hearts so that we may not turn away from Him.

Discuss: What have you done (said or thought) recently that you knew no one else would find out about? How does it make you feel to know that the righteous God of the universe saw (or heard) you?

Pray: Bow in prayer and confess any of those unseen and unheard thoughts, attitudes and actions now.

Pray that your marriage would be characterized by the benefits of fearing God.

WHY YOU NEED THE SPIRIT
(PART ONE)

Do not get drunk with wine, for that is dissipation,
but be filled with the Spirit.

EPHESIANS 5:18

$\mathcal{M}$ost Christians agree that the Holy Spirit is the third Person of the Trinity. We referred to Him as the Holy Ghost when I was a little boy growing up in a church that strictly used the *King James Version* of the Bible. And for a long time I could only imagine something like the cartoon character Casper the Ghost—floating through walls like a puff of smoke.

For years I referred to the Holy Ghost as an "it." But the Holy Ghost Jesus talks about is a Person. He was sent, not only to glorify Christ, but also to be our Counselor, Adviser, Advocate, Defender, Director and Guide.

In short, if you are interested in living the abundant life Jesus promised, the Holy Spirit is vital. Just think of all the sermons you've heard on the Christian life. Think of all the books you've read about marriage.

If you try in your own power to obey God and follow all that advice, you will fail—period. It's impossible. You need God's power that He promises when you have yielded yourself to the Holy Spirit.

Look again at Ephesians 5:18. Have you ever wondered why Paul put being drunk with wine in opposition to being filled with the Spirit? Because he wanted to help his readers understand what being filled means. When you are drunk with wine, you are controlled by alcohol. The same is true in a positive sense when you are filled with the Spirit: You allow the Spirit to control you.

No relationship, marriage or family will ever be all that God intends unless its members are experiencing God at work in their lives through the enabling work of the Holy Spirit.

Discuss: Think back over your married life and family. How has the Holy Spirit been your Counselor, Adviser, Advocate, Defender, Director and Guide?

Pray: Together ask God to help you learn how to allow the Holy Spirit to control your lives.

THE HOLY SPIRIT IS OUR
COUNSELOR, ADVISER,
ADVOCATE, DEFENDER,
DIRECTOR AND GUIDE.

WHY YOU NEED THE SPIRIT
(PART TWO)

Be subject to one another in the fear of Christ.

EPHESIANS 5:21

I find it revealing that Paul discusses the Holy Spirit (see Eph. 5:18-21) just before moving into a practical discussion of family relationships (see 5:22—6:4). Obviously, a clear result of being filled with the Spirit is to have a submissive spirit. Men and women are to submit to each other and to serve each other's needs.

Each of us needs to defeat selfishness. On many occasions I have a desire to be angry at Barbara. Yet, at the same time, I realize that my life is a temple of God, that the Holy Spirit lives in me with the same power that raised Christ from the dead. The Spirit helps me control my temper, my impatience and my desire to say things I would later regret.

In marriage, there is to be mutual submission: A woman yields to the leadership of a man who denies himself in order to love his wife as Christ loves the Church. What a mystery this is! The husband is still the leader, but he submits his life to his mate.

In this type of situation, the woman's responsibility of submission takes on an entirely new meaning. Any husband who is living out Paul's instructions in Ephesians 5 could never treat his wife as a second-class citizen or with chauvinist disregard for her needs and feelings. That is the farthest thing from Paul's (and God's) mind.

As you and your mate ask God to empower you with the Holy Spirit, His fruit will become a growing, increasing part of your life together. And as the God of peace and harmony fills your hearts and takes up residency in your marriage, you will experience the oneness and intimacy that only He can provide.

Discuss: What evidence could you, as a husband, present to show that you consistently love your wife as Christ loves the Church? What evidence could you, as a wife, present to show that you are being submissive to your husband?

Pray: Pray that the Holy Spirit would give you not only an understanding of your unique roles and responsibilities in marriage but also the ability to subject your lives to each other.

PULLING WEEDS AND PLANTING SEEDS
(PART ONE)

Behold, the sower went out to sow. And other seed
fell among the thorns, and the thorns came up and
choked it, and it yielded no crop.

MARK 4:3,7

*M*aybe you've experienced the hope of planting a new garden or lawn. You had a snapshot in your mind of what it would look like—high expectations of vegetable-laden plants or of your neighbor's looking enviously at your lush green lawn. But you discovered that good gardens and thick, carpetlike lawns don't grow naturally—weeds do.

Pulling weeds and planting seeds. That's the story of life. We are individual lots on which either weeds of selfishness or fruit of the Holy Spirit grow and flourish. Jesus warned that the soil of our hearts is the most valuable acreage on planet Earth.

In Mark 4, Jesus taught the parable of the sower and soils to His disciples. Christ said that spiritual fruitfulness or barrenness depends upon the type of soil that receives the seed of God's Word.

Jesus warned of the choking influence of thorns—pesky prickly weeds that squeeze the life out of fruit-producing seedlings.

"The worries of the world" (Mark 4:19) are the first weeds of which Jesus warned. To me, it's easy to feel choked by the worries of the world when I'm pulled in different directions by competing priorities and by the distractions of a busy life. A full schedule of good things that crowd out the best—like time in the morning spent in prayer and in Scripture—causes me to focus too much on the world instead of on my relationship with God.

What distracts you? What pulls you in a direction you know is unfruitful? Some people are distracted and worried about what others think about them. They are preoccupied with pleasing men and gaining their approval. Still others are pulled by their insecurities, trying to find significance in achieving and performing.

Good marriages and families don't grow naturally—weeds do. That's why it's so important that we listen to the words of the Master Gardener, Jesus Christ.

Discuss: What things distract you from a life of fruitfulness? What "worries of the world" influence you?

Pray: Ask God to use your mate to keep you accountable to live by God's priorities.

THE SOIL OF OUR
HEARTS IS THE MOST
VALUABLE ACREAGE
ON PLANET EARTH.

PULLING WEEDS AND PLANTING SEEDS
(PART TWO)

And others are the ones on whom seed was sown among the thorns; these are the ones who have heard the word, and the worries of the world, and the deceitfulness of riches, and the desires for other things enter in and choke the word, and it becomes unfruitful.

MARK 4:18-19

The second weed Jesus spoke of in Mark 4 is "the deceitfulness of riches." Maybe you're thinking, *Hey, I don't want to be poor. I'd rather take my chances with handling being rich and whatever deceit comes with it! Wealth isn't so bad.*

I remember the year we held our first Urban Family Conference in Harlem. There was no veneer of wealth in Harlem—just unveiled hopelessness. You could see it and feel it.

But when I arrived home after the Harlem conference, I couldn't help but notice the clean and prosperous suburban neighborhoods of Little Rock, Arkansas. Then it hit me: Many of the people in Little Rock were just hiding their hopelessness beneath the veneer of their prosperity. In reality they needed the light of Jesus Christ just as much as those people in Harlem.

Wealth is a deceptive weed that takes over our lives and chokes out our responsiveness to God. The following question will help you measure the deceit of wealth in your life: Would you be willing to give up the safety of your job and salary and invest your life in full-time vocational ministry if the Lord called you to? If you're not willing, then you may need to pull some weeds of deception.

Beware of prosperous times—they can be deadly, numbing the heart's response to God's direction for your life. Materialism may be the number one weed that is choking out spiritual revival and awakening in America.

Discuss: In what ways have you seen materialism deceive you or others into believing they do not have a need for God?

Pray: Regardless of your income, ask God to keep you free from the deceiving clutches of wealth and materialism.

PULLING WEEDS AND PLANTING SEEDS
(PART THREE)

*And the desires for other things enter in and choke
the word, and it becomes unfruitful.*

MARK 4:19

The final thorn, or weed, that hinders fruitfulness in our lives is "the desire for other things." Some of these weeds are easily spotted, such as sexual lust, an addiction to pornography, or perversions. But other cravings aren't so easily identifiable: food, clothing, jewelry, car, job, salary, a hobby or sport, or even the location or kind of house we live in. Any desire that drives us, controls our thinking or preoccupies our minds can be a weed that hinders growth in our lives.

One good way to spot a weed is to check your conversations: What are you most excited about? What subjects do you discuss with others? What preoccupies your thoughts daily? Is it something honorable?

I guess what scares me about all these weeds is their potential for multiplication. When I was a kid, I used to take great delight in breaking off the stem of a dandelion that proudly held a cluster of seeds. A stiff breeze or the slightest whiff of breath would instantly launch a jillion of those tiny angel-hair parachutes. Now as I fight the spread of these wind-borne warriors, I can't help but wonder how many dandelions there are in just one of those seed puffs?

Letting just one weed grow freely in your life could result in a crop failure of good fruit. Thorns and thistles reduce the yield of the harvest. A friend of mine who grows popcorn once told me that weeds left unattended can cut the harvest by as much as 40 to 60 percent. I couldn't help but think about how I need to get serious about pulling, poisoning and plowing under the weeds in my own life.

I wish I had some high-powered, nuclear herbicide to help you instantly eradicate weeds from your life. The reality is that all soil has weed seeds. Lives do too. What you and I need is a personal visit from the Master Gardener and His hoe.

Discuss: What desires "for other things" preoccupy your thoughts on a daily basis?

Pray: Ask God to do some fresh cultivation in the soil of your heart.

ALL SOIL HAS WEED SEEDS;
LIVES DO TOO.

OUR MOST MEMORABLE CHRISTMAS GIFT
(PART ONE)

*Present your bodies a living and holy
sacrifice, acceptable to God.*

ROMANS 12:1

*B*arbara and I were once asked, "What is the most memorable Christmas gift you've ever given or received?" Instantly our minds raced backward over invisible tracks and skidded to a stop at the same intersection: our first Christmas together as a couple, in 1972.

Our Christmas tree that year was sparsely decorated with a dozen red ornaments. The small living room was quiet but warm. Only a few presents lay scattered under the Scotch pine.

Neither of us has any recollection of what prompted us, but evidently the Spirit of God wanted us to dedicate and commemorate our new life together in Jesus Christ. So we decided that before we would give each other our gifts, we would first give God the most valued gift we possessed: our lives.

The kitchen table became Barbara's altar, while I sat on the borrowed couch. Each of us, individually, spent some time writing out the title deeds to our lives.

It was a time of counting the cost of being a committed follower of Jesus Christ. It meant relinquishing all rights and ownership of our lives to God. It was a practical application of Romans 12:1-2, which urges us to commit our lives totally to the Lord.

That bare-bones honesty with God wasn't easy. We wrote down all that we desired, all the things we thought were important, and we said we wanted to give them to Him. Then, folding and placing those two sheets of paper in an envelope, we wrote on the outside "To God, Our Father."

We sealed the envelope, and then we verbalized together in prayer what had already taken place privately on our sheets of paper.

There were no bells. No angelic choirs. No blinding light. Just the firm confidence that what we had done was right.

Eighteen years later we retrieved those documents from our safety deposit box and read them. And in the next devotion I'll show you what we found.

Discuss: Have you ever written out a title deed to your life? What would prevent you from giving God total control of your life?

Pray: Pray that you would each be able to whole-heartedly give your life completely to Him.

OUR MOST MEMORABLE CHRISTMAS GIFT
(PART TWO)

[God] is able to do exceedingly abundantly beyond all that we ask or think, according to the power that works within us.

EPHESIANS 3:20

*I*t was fascinating to read, 18 years later, the earnest commitment we had made as a young couple. At the top of our pages was a similar statement, and then came our lists (the following are partial lists):

Contract with God

I hereby give all rights to God of the following things that I want:

Dennis
Nice big house with workshop, office
To ski well
Nice furniture and things

Sharp clothes
Security
Easygoing job
Success in ministry and speaking ability
Stay healthy
A healthy, big family—several boys
Barbara

Barbara
Children—at least one boy and one girl
Dennis
To live to see my children grow up
To be settled and stable
To be an outstanding couple and family

Reading the lists on those two pages, Barbara and I were immediately stunned by two things. First, we noticed how silly and shallow some of the things were that we deemed valuable and difficult to give up to God. I was struck by how much I was preoccupied with material things. Looking back over our years together, I found it fascinating how God had continuously sought to wean us from that which is perishable and to replace our values with the imperishable: people and His Word.

Second, we were surprised at how much more God has given us than what we gave up. We immediately thought of Ephesians 3:20. Both of us feel we sacrificed nothing and have gained far more than we ever dreamed of.

Discuss: Get alone with God and make your own list of things that are most important to you. Prayerfully formalize a contract with God, giving Him total ownership and rights to your life. Sign and date your document.

Pray: Ask God to give you discernment about your true priorities in life.

COURAGE MEANS
MOVING FORWARD IN SPITE
OF YOUR FEARS TO
FACE THE TASK YOU'VE
BEEN GIVEN.

PRIVATE BATTLEFIELDS

Be strong, and let your heart take courage,
all you who hope in the LORD.

PSALM 31:24

*I*t was June 1994, and magazines and newspapers were awash with stories and pictures about D day. Thousands of veterans revisited Normandy to recall that heroic battle and to honor their fallen comrades. These soldiers who bravely invaded enemy beaches had more than guns, bullets and provisions on their backs—they carried the outcome of World War II on their shoulders.

One picture will be forever etched in my mind. It was a German photograph of a Nazi machine gunner perched in a well-protected bunker above Omaha Beach. His advantage must have been merciless. Undoubtedly, he mowed down hundreds of our young men as they sought to make it across the beach to the protection of the hills and cliffs.

I've thought often of the fear those men faced as they lunged out of the safety of their landing craft and into the foaming tide. Bullets delivering death popped the water as the soldiers fought the surf and pushed onto the beach.

Some people think that courage means having no fear, but I disagree. Courage means moving forward in spite of your fears to face the task you've been given. And that's what those men did.

Today we're engaged in another battle—for the family. There's a big difference in this battle though. It's being fought in private—in the hearts of men and women and in the homes where they attempt, day after day, to build loving relationships.

Every day they make choices between denying themselves and following God's plan to love and serve each other, and fulfilling their own selfish desires. And when those battles of the heart are lost, we see the wreckage—divorce, abuse and neglect, which produce shattered lives and an astonishing number of young people who have entered the world without the ability to make strong and courageous moral choices.

Often we approach these choices with the same type of trepidation that those men faced on the beaches of Normandy. We forget the God who calls us to hope in Him. But the battle for the family will be won if you and I decide to conquer the battlefront that is before us.

Discuss: What are some difficult battles you are facing in your family right now?

Pray: Spend time asking God to give you the courage to face the battlefronts you are facing and the ability to put your hope in Him.

TOWARD A NEW BREED OF MEN

While we look not at the things which are seen, but at the things which are not seen; for the things which are seen are temporal, but the things which are not seen are eternal.

2 CORINTHIANS 4:18

Why do Fortune 500 companies pay such huge salaries to their top executives? Because they know that leadership makes a difference.

As a husband and father, your leadership will make a difference in your family. Oh, your wife and children may survive from day to day, but are they heading anywhere? Are they growing in Christlike character? Are they focusing on what is important?

There is no question why so many marriages and families are in trouble. Too many men are functioning only as material providers. We need a new breed of men who can appreciate and expend energy, time and—most important—focused attention on the spiritual aspect of family life.

We need a new breed of men who have the ability to focus on the unseen—the eternal—as well as the seen. Men who will say no to making more bucks when doing so means sacrificing their families. A new breed who will ask themselves, with every decision they make, *How will this affect the relationships within my family?*

We need a new breed of men who will recognize they need to leave something to posterity that will outlive the financial inheritances they may leave for their children: *proven character.* A new breed of men who realize that to succeed in the eyes of men but fail in the eyes of God is the ultimate failure.

As Peter Marshall, the late United States Senate chaplain, is known to have said, "It is better to fail in a cause that will ultimately succeed than to succeed in a cause that will ultimately fail."

Will you take upon yourself the challenge Albert Einstein gave a group of young scientists? While addressing this highly motivated group of young men, he said, "Gentlemen, try not to become men of success. But rather, try to become men of value."

Discuss: What material things do you hope to leave to your children? What specific spiritual values do you hope to instill in them? Which of these "keepsakes" is more important?

Pray: Imagine your children as grown and established in their own families. Pray for what each one will become.

MOST IMPORTANT, MY FATHER
TAUGHT ME ABOUT CHARACTER.
HE DID WHAT WAS RIGHT, EVEN
WHEN NO ONE WAS LOOKING.

"HE WAS A GOOD MAN"

Then when he had come and witnessed the grace of God, he rejoiced and began to encourage them all with resolute heart to remain true to the Lord; for he was a good man.

ACTS 11:23-24

What memories do you have of your father? What legacy did he leave you?

One way to learn more about yourself is to think back on your father's character. I enjoy doing this because my dad had such an influence on who I am today.

My dad uniquely blended a no-nonsense attitude and discipline with a subtle sense of humor. He was a quiet and private man. He didn't seem to need many words to get the job done.

His countenance commanded respect. In fact, eight boys had personality transformations when they graduated from the third-grade Sunday School class to my dad's fourth-grade class. Paper airplanes were grounded and the boys sat up straight, listening dutifully to the lesson.

I recall the easy chair that used to carry the shape of his exhausted form. It was as he read the evening paper that I usually planned my assault on him. I'm sure I nearly pestered my weary dad to death while asking him to play catch.

Hook Rainey, they used to call him. The tall lefty got his nickname from his curve ball—a pitch so crooked it mystified batters. When he threw that patented knuckler, the entire front yard was filled with laughter—his and mine. I always loved to hear him laugh. Somehow it told me that everything was secure.

When I was three or so, he went hunting in Colorado and "bagged" a fierce teddy bear. He staged the "action" on film and brought the "slain" beast back to me. My kids now play with that well-worn 45-year-old black-and-white bear.

I watched Dad look after the needs of his mother—he used to visit her three or four times a week. He modeled what it meant to honor one's parents. Most important, he taught me about character. He did what was right, even when no one was looking. I never heard him lie, and his eyes always demanded the same truth in return. The mental image of his character still fuels and energizes my life today.

Discuss: In what specific ways do you hope to influence your children? How does your life match up to the ideals and values of Scripture?

Pray: Ask God to give you the strength and wisdom to be godly parents.

FAITHFUL IN LITTLE THINGS

He who is faithful in a very little thing is faithful also in much; and he who is unrighteous in a very little thing is unrighteous also in much.

LUKE 16:10

*A*re you trustworthy? Can others count on you? Do you want to know how to be original in a culture of copycats? Do you want to be a part of a vanishing breed in today's generation?

If so, then become a person who is *faithful*. You know, a person who follows through; whom others can count on whether things are rough or smooth; whose word is good on the little stuff, as well as the mammoth, gargantuan tasks; the kind of person who promises to call—and does so—on time; who says something will get done and does it—exactly like you have asked for it to be done.

Are you known as a faithful person? If you are, then here are a few of the words that can be used to describe you: "trustworthy," "dependable," "reliable," "true-blue" and "responsible." All of these words are saturated with one recurring theme: *character*. Character quietly yet convincingly says, "You can count on me—at any cost!"

If you want to find a biblical example of someone who was faithful in little things, turn to the last chapters of Genesis. As you read through the story of Joseph, you see a man who was considered trustworthy:

- He was given responsibility to shepherd his father's flocks "while he was still a youth" (Gen. 37:2).
- After he was sold into slavery by his brothers, he ended up in the house of Potiphar, where he performed his duties well enough to be appointed overseer of all that Potiphar owned (see 39:5).
- He refused the amorous advances of Potiphar's wife. Unfortunately, he was thrown into prison when she lied and said he had tried to seduce her (see 39:7-20).
- His character in prison was so strong that the chief jailer placed him in charge of all the prisoners (see 39:21-23).
- After interpreting Pharaoh's dream, he was taken from prison and made a ruler in Egypt, second in power only to Pharaoh (see 41:38-41).

Joseph never sought to move up in responsibility. He was faithful to fulfill his responsibilities and content to allow God to give him more.

We all have ambitions of some sort, but sometimes I wonder if our ambitions are in the right area. In Mark 10:35-

45, Jesus said the greatest ambition is to be the slave of all—a servant.

Do you want to be a leader? Then you've got to be a servant.

Discuss: Are you faithful in little things or do you often seem to neglect them?

Pray: Ask God to build in you a spirit of faithfulness. If you desire to have additional responsibilities, ask Him to give you the desire to serve others.

HUMILITY IS TO
KNOW GOD AND TO
KNOW WHO YOU ARE IN
RELATION TO HIM.

THE PROBLEM WITH PRIDE

When pride comes, then comes dishonor,
but with the humble is wisdom.

PROVERBS 11:2

℘ride," said Soviet dissident Aleksandr Solzhenitsyn, "grows in the human heart like lard on a pig."[1] Pride is one of the few things that can grow without any sustenance in the human heart. And although it seems to flourish more visibly in some people, all the human race suffers under its malignant grip.

Pride has many different faces. It can try to demand control: "I want it my way"; "I want to be my own god, run my own show and submit to no one."

It can be seen in the stubborn—what the Scriptures call "stiff-necked" (Exod. 32:9, *KJV*) or "hardhearted" (Ezek. 3:7, *KJV*). And it is most easily detected in those who carry themselves in an arrogant manner. When I was a kid, we used to call kids like this stuck-up, snooty, snobbish, conceited or cocky.

Well-known evangelist Dwight L. Moody described how God deals with pride: "God sends no one away empty except those who are full of themselves." Daily I attempt to put "self" to death and ask that Jesus Christ might have unhindered access to every area of my life. Then, as I am tempted to get angry because things didn't go my way, I'm reminded that to give in to pride is death.

So what is the way of humility? To know God and to know who you are in relation to Him. Phillip Brooks once said, "The true way to be humble is not to stoop until you are smaller than yourself, but to stand at your real height against some higher nature that will show you what the real smallness of your greatness is."[2]

My pride wants to say, "I don't need God—I'm perfectly happy without Him." But what amazes me is that real happiness comes when I'm willing to humble myself and do what He wills with my life. The process may be painful, but it also brings real joy.

Discuss: In what areas of your life do you feel self-sufficient?

Pray: Pray that God would show you the joy that comes with humility.

Notes

1. Aleksandr Solzhenitsyn, *The Gulag Archipelago* (New York: Perennial/HarperCollins Publishers, 2002), n.p.
2. Phillip Brooks, quoted in Elizabeth Skoglund, *Burning Out for God* (Downers Grove, IL: InterVarsity Press, 1988), p. 11.

GRIPES, GRUMBLES AND GROUCHES
(PART ONE)

Do all things without grumbling or disputing.
PHILIPPIANS 2:14

*D*o you ever get annoyed with the complaining around your house? I do. Over the years the rooms of the Rainey household have resounded with gripes about many things:

- Who gets to sit where at the dinner table
- Who gets to sit in the front seat on the way to school or church
- Toilets that aren't flushed
- Toys that populate the floor
- Tubs littered with dolls, boats, bottles and melting bars of soap
- Who has to clean up the dishes
- Whether the food for (pick a meal) looks, feels or tastes appetizing

It became so bad one year that we all memorized Philippians 2:14: "Do all things without grumbling or disputing." That helped.

Like sulfuric acid, complaining can eat away at whatever it splashes on. Complaining corrodes joy and dissolves good attitudes. Spiritually, it's dangerous and deadly.

If you have a problem with grumbling, you're not alone. The Old Testament book of Numbers could easily be renamed the Grumbler Chronicles. The children of Israel grumbled against Moses, Aaron and God. They didn't like manna, so they complained: "Manna for breakfast, lunch and dinner! Is this all we get, this manna?" (see Num. 11).

So God gave them quail instead. They had quail boiled and broiled until they were sick of it.

Can you empathize with them? A little complaining is understandable, isn't it?

But the complaining by the children of Israel wasn't a trivial matter, and God didn't view it lightly. He had delivered them from Egypt and was providing for them daily. They were just plain ungrateful.

I wonder what we would find if we performed open-heart surgery on a complainer. Exploratory surgery would reveal that grumbling can be a form of heart disease, rebellion against authority. It also shows a loss of perspective, a failure to remember who is in control. It's an attitude that questions, "Does God really know what's best for me?"

Discuss: What are you trying to do when you grumble and complain? What are your children trying to do when they gripe?

Pray: If appropriate, have each family member specifically confess the sin of grumbling, and in prayer give thanks to God for at least three things.

LIKE SULFURIC ACID,
COMPLAINING CAN EAT AWAY AT
WHATEVER IT SPLASHES ON.

GRIPES, GRUMBLES AND GROUCHES
(PART TWO)

*These are grumblers, finding fault, following after
their own lusts; they speak arrogantly, flattering people
for the sake of gaining an advantage.*

JUDE 16

Griping and complaining are vocal amplifiers of one's heart
attitude. What's the solution for us gripers?

First, *realize that complaining is dangerous.* While many
Christian leaders have fallen into immorality, I wonder how
many more Christians have been declared unusable by God
because of their complaining? For many of us, that snare is
the temptation to gripe, grumble and complain against God
(see 1 Cor. 9:24—10:13).

Second, *remember that God knows what He's doing.* Joseph
knew this truth. Scripture doesn't record a single complaint
from his lips even though he was tossed into a pit by his
brothers, sold into slavery, unjustly accused of fooling
around with Potiphar's wife, thrown into prison and forgotten by a friend he had helped.

What was the secret of his complaint-free life? The answer is in Genesis 45:5-8, where we find Joseph, now the governor of Egypt, addressing his starving brothers. Three times in four verses Joseph, in essence, says, "God sent me here." His perspective came as a result of an uncommon faith in an omnipotent God. Joseph grasped the truth that God is in control and knows what He is doing.

Third, *put away past complaints that may become bitterness.* If you have a complaint against a brother, go to him in private and clear the slate.

Fourth, *"in everything give thanks"* (1 Thess. 5:18). Jesus gave the disciples a test of their faith by putting them in a little boat on a big sea during an even bigger raging storm. The disciples complained that they were perishing when instead they should have acknowledged God's sovereignty and trusted Him.

God wants you to see Him in the midst of your circumstances, to trust Him even when you do not see the outcome clearly presented in front of you. That is true faith. It is knowing that His Word is truer than anything you can think, see or feel.

Discuss: Are you satisfied with what God has provided for you today (your mate, your children, your circumstances)? Does God know what He is doing in your life?

Pray: Give thanks right now for where God has you as individuals and as a family. Be specific as you thank Him for your circumstances.

COMPLACENCY VERSUS COMMITMENT

Therefore let him who thinks he stands take heed lest he fall.

1 CORINTHIANS 10:12

We need to make certain that marriage is divorceproof. Pastor and author Chuck Swindoll asks a great question: "Are there any termites in your troth?" One of those termites could be complacency.

First Corinthians 10:12 offers a formidable warning to the one who thinks this infestation of termites can't reach into his or her marriage. How many ministers, missionaries and laymen have fallen into affairs and divorce after allowing romantic complacency to settle in?

We need to resurrect the true meaning of commitment. In this age of lite beer, lite syrup and lite salad dressing, it's no wonder we exhibit lite commitment, too. But for a Christian, commitment is a sacred vow and promise to God. It's two people who hang in there during the best and worst of times and who won't quit. It's a husband and wife who find working through problems much more rewarding than walking out.

We need to pass on to our children the real definition of commitment while continually exposing the lies that their peers and the media propagate. A person who does not understand his or her ultimate accountability to God has little reason to fulfill a vow, or commitment, to another human being.

There's another type of complacency we need to address: the acceptance of the demise of marriages besides our own. A growing number of Christians, upon hearing of the hurt and anguish of their friends, do not reach for their Bibles but instead hastily offer a parachute and say, "Bail out!" Or they simply sit by, saying and doing nothing. They just let it happen. Hey, I understand. When there's only a slim thread of hope, what are you going to do?

You and I have got to go to the guy who just left his family and tell him it's not going to be that easy. He can't just walk out on them. And that woman in our Sunday School class? She can't leave her husband for that other guy and think things will be business as usual. We've got to plead, beg and pray with them—and get them some help.

Discuss: What kind of commitment do you and your mate have? Is it lite, or is it full strength? Do you know any couples who are struggling in their marriages? What can you do to encourage them?

Pray: Reaffirm your wedding vows to one another in prayer by acknowledging your absolute commitment to your spouse. And keep praying with me that God will purge our land of divorce.

IS YOUR COMMITMENT LITE OR FULL STRENGTH?

PLEASING YOUR MATE

*Now we who are strong ought to bear the weaknesses
of those without strength and not just please ourselves.
Let each of us please his neighbor for his good, to his
edification. For even Christ did not please Himself.*

ROMANS 15:1-3

I am convinced that great marriages and great families are rooted in self-denial. In a truly biblical, Christian marriage, both people are willing to give up their lives for one another in order to love their mate properly.

During the early years of our marriage, I remember looking into the rearview mirror of the car as I pulled out of the driveway to go fishing with several of our children one Saturday. Barbara was standing on the porch, left with a couple of kids in diapers, while I went off to the lake with the older kids to have a good time.

While I was sitting in that boat, not catching anything, I continued to think about Barbara. I thought, *You know, I'm pleasing myself, but I haven't done a good job of pleasing her.* I realized that I needed to give up some of my hobbies for a while in order to please her and reduce her burden.

In our nation's economy, we usually determine the value of a piece of merchandise or a service by how much we have to give up, or sacrifice, to gain it. If my son wishes to buy a new basketball, it will cost him a couple of weekends of freedom in order to complete enough chores to earn the money to pay for it.

In a similar fashion, your mate often interprets how much you love or value him or her by how much you are willing to sacrifice for him or her.

For the woman trying to please her husband, it has often been said that the way to a man's heart is through his stomach. Why not cook the foods he enjoys? Be careful not to become his mother, feeding him only what is good for him. Spoil him a little.

A husband can please his wife by finding out what her number one need is and then by helping to meet that need if he can. It may be as simple as taking a walk and talking with her or as complex as confronting a child that has her under his or her control.

The main concern here is to do the right thing: Please your spouse.

Discuss: How can Romans 15:1-3 be applied to your marriage? Take the pulse of your heart to please one another. Write down and then discuss the three things your spouse could do that would truly please you.

Pray: Ask God to give you the ability to focus on pleasing your mate rather than yourself.

THE LAW OF GIVING

Give, and it will be given to you; good measure,
pressed down, shaken together, running over, they will
pour into your lap. For by your standard of measure it
will be measured to you in return.

LUKE 6:38

Christianity is full of apparent paradoxes, including one that Jesus teaches us: If we give, we will receive. Somehow a transfer takes place so that when we give, we are enriched. We are not depleted, even if we do not see it or feel it at the time.

This law of giving applies to many areas of life, but it is especially relevant to self-esteem. As one woman wrote in a letter to Barbara and me, "I have realized that in giving of myself, I am actually getting in return a spouse who feels good about himself, which then makes me feel good about myself."

The world whispers to us, "You can give away only what you have. Wait until your own needs are met. Then you will be able to reach out to others and really give." But is that what Jesus meant when He said "Give"?

We think not. Why? Perhaps Jesus knew that nobody ever reaches that point where all needs are met.

Perhaps you get tired of giving. You may be thinking, *You don't know my mate. I don't want to give this time.* I can understand a little bit—what spouse hasn't had his or her moments. But when truth is not ruling in your life, feelings are. Acting on negative feelings will not build your mate's self-image or your marriage—it will only tear down what you've already built.

Even if you feel you've given and given and given for years, please don't give up. Your mate needs you more than you realize. God sees, and He will reward you.

Eighteenth-century theologian F. B. Meyer said, "He is the richest man in the esteem of the world who has gotten most. He is the richest man in the esteem of heaven who has given most."

Where do you want to be the richest?

Discuss: How can you begin applying the law of giving in your marriage this week? Write down two or three ways.

Pray: Ask God to help you make daily choices to put aside your own selfish desires and have a giving heart.

WHAT DID JESUS MEAN WHEN HE SAID "GIVE"?

ACCOUNTABILITY IN MARRIAGE

*Two are better than one because they have a good
return for their labor. For if either of them falls,
the one will lift up his companion.*

ECCLESIASTES 4:9-10

I believe that if there is anything that can ensure and incorporate character—godly character—in your life and mine, it is accountability. And more than to anyone else, I have determined that I will be accountable to my wife, Barbara.

Marriage is a perfect arena for accountability. As you and your mate face continuing pressures and stress, it's best to handle life in duet, not solo. Two can always see more clearly than one. Your mate can detect blind spots that you may not be able to see.

Barbara and I practice accountability in our marriage in a variety of areas. One area is our *schedule*. We try to help each other make good decisions by monitoring each other's workload and schedule. When somebody invites me to speak somewhere, I say, "I can't give you an answer now. My wife and I have agreed that I don't take any speaking engagements without talking with her." And so we do talk about it, and Barbara helps me say no when I need to.

Another area is *money and values*. We constantly check our personal values. What is really important to each of us? Why are we doing what we are doing? Where do we dare not lose? What do we spend our money on and how does that reflect our values?

A third area concerns *fidelity*. Some years ago I led a Bible study that included several new Christians. During those studies, Barbara began to sense that one of the men was increasingly friendly toward her. At first she thought she was imagining things, so she kept it to herself. When she finally told me what was happening, I could see unmistakable relief spread across her face. What had been her personal secret quickly evaporated as we discussed her feelings together.

Fortunately, Barbara's admirer never tried going beyond being friendly. But looking back on that incident, we see that it was a test for both of us. It reaffirmed our commitment to each other as we stood together against a potential threat to our marriage.

Your spouse should be your number one accountability partner.

Discuss: Do you feel free to be accountable to your mate? Why or why not? You may want to discuss accountability with your spouse.

Pray: Pray that God would use accountability to your mate to help you and your spouse grow closer to Christ and preserve your marriage.

ACCOUNTABILITY TO OTHERS

Iron sharpens iron, so one man sharpens another.

PROVERBS 27:17

While your mate should be your primary accountability partner, there also is great benefit in getting sharpened by other godly Christians. If you want to see some significant growth in your spiritual maturity, choosing to become accountable may be the most important decision you could make.

Here are four steps you can take to become accountable:

1. *Determine your needs.* What are the two or three things that seem to entangle you more than anything else? Is it finances? Lustful thoughts? Overeating? Not spending enough time with the Lord?

2. *Select a mature Christian—of the same sex—who would have the courage to speak the truth and ask you tough questions.* This should not be someone who would fear your rejection, someone who has a

weakness in the same area or someone you feel you can manipulate or control. This is especially important if you are strong willed or have a powerful personality.

3. *Approach this person and ask him or her to keep you accountable.* Here is what you might say: "Bill, I have a problem and I really need your help in an area of my life. I need for you to love me through this and hold my feet to the fire but not be judgmental. Because, Bill, I really need to get victory over this."

4. *Meet with this person on a regular basis to set measurable goals and to allow him or her to ask you how you're doing.* Agree to a list of questions he or she will ask you: "Frank, have you written out a budget yet?" "Why not?" "When will you do it?" And here's a powerful one: "Have you lied to me at all today?"

If you're trying to mature in Christ and gain victory over sin by yourself, you're missing the point! Praise God that He has given us the Body of Christ to strengthen us, encourage us and keep us accountable!

Discuss: What are your greatest needs—ones that would lead you to find an accountability partner? Who are potential accountability partners you could approach?

Pray: Ask God to lead you to people whom He can use to sharpen you.

PUTTING DOWN THE
BURDEN OF A GRUDGE
CAN MAKE US ABSOLUTELY
LIGHTHEARTED.

TOO HEAVY TO CARRY

*And be kind to one another, tender-hearted, forgiving each
other, just as God in Christ also has forgiven you.*

EPHESIANS 4:32

Someone once asked, "Did you know the longer you carry
a grudge, the heavier it gets?" Refusing to forgive those who
wrong us can be a wearying weight on the soul.

On the other hand, when we choose to forgive, we shed
a huge burden we simply don't need to carry through life. It
can make us absolutely lighthearted to put down the burden of a grudge.

What can you do to keep from carrying grudges and an
unforgiving spirit through life?

For one thing, *clarify your inner occupation.* Do you want
to make judging others your spiritual career path? Jesus
said, "Do not judge lest you be judged" (Matt. 7:1), indicat-
ing that pursuing the occupation of judge will boomerang
on you.

Judging, just like taking vengeance, belongs to God, not
to people: "Vengeance is mine; I will repay, saith the Lord"
(Rom. 12:19, *KJV*). Even after David had committed adultery
with Bathsheba and had her husband killed, he said to God,

"Against Thee, Thee only, I have sinned" (Ps. 51:4).

Since God makes the rules, He is the only true Judge. People who wrong others really wrong God more than others. Relieve yourself of the responsibility that actually belongs only to God.

Giving up the judgeship means you also *relieve yourself of the responsibility of punishment.* Forgiving someone doesn't necessarily mean we forget immediately or even completely, but it does mean we no longer hold a private grudge that desires to punish or see that person punished.

You can also avoid carrying grudges by *resolving conflicts as they occur.* "Do not let the sun go down on your anger" (Eph. 4:26). Which would you rather face—the short-term emotional pain of asking another to forgive you for your anger, or the lifelong cancerous feeling of bitterness you carry because you won't resolve the conflict? It's your choice.

Discuss: How would people who know you best describe you? Do you tend to carry grudges? Evaluate if you are carrying any grudges at home, at work or at church.

Pray: Pray that the forgiving grace of God you've experienced in your own life will also characterize your attitude toward those who wrong you.

STAYING IN FOCUS

See that no one repays another with evil for evil,
but always seek after that which is good for one
another and for all men.

1 T H E S S A L O N I A N S   5 : 1 5

$\mathcal{A}$s we mentioned in yesterday's reading, it's important to resolve conflicts as they occur. When you resolve a conflict, you must stay focused—on the right things. Take this pop quiz on marital conflict and learn what those right things are. C'mon, be honest, and discuss your answers with your spouse.

1. *Do you stick to one issue during a conflict or do you focus on many issues?* Don't save up a series of complaints and let your mate have them all at once. Deal with one thing at a time.

2. *Do you focus on your spouse's behavior rather than attack his or her character?* Don't try to make your mate feel like an enemy or the bad guy. And avoid sweeping statements like "You are so forgetful" or "This is just like you!"

3. *Do you focus on the facts rather than judging the motives?* If your partner forgets to make an important call,

deal with the consequences of what you both have to do next rather than saying, "You don't really care about this, do you?"

4. *Do you focus on understanding your mate rather than on who wins or loses?* When your mate confronts you, listen carefully to what is said and what isn't said. It may be, for example, that your spouse is upset about something else that happened during the day and you're just getting the brunt of that pressure. In other words, you may not be the problem. Your mate may just need to vent some pent-up frustrations and feelings. While that may not always be fair, part of being a loving partner is being willing to listen and to help.

5. *When you're confronted, do you listen with a teachable spirit or do you justify your behavior?* Be willing to hear and receive the truth when you are confronted. The natural thing to do is to employ a defense lawyer's tactics. Fire the lawyer; hire the teachable student.

6. *Do you usually give your spouse the benefit of the doubt or do you use phrases like "You always do . . ." or "You never do . . ."?* Generalizations are seldom true—avoid using them in your marriage.

Discuss: Recall an argument when you probably wanted to win more than you wanted to solve the problem. Why can staying focused in a confrontation be so difficult?

Pray: Each of you pick one of the six questions that you struggle with, and pray together that God will enable you to do what He wants in your next conflict.

THERE'S NOTHING
LIKE A GOOD THUMP
TO REVEAL THE NATURE
OF THE HEART.

DAY 26

THE THUMP TEST

The good man out of the good treasure of his heart brings forth what is good; and the evil man out of the evil treasure brings forth what is evil; for his mouth speaks from that which fills his heart.

LUKE 6:45

Max Lucado once wrote about the way a potter checks his work. When he pulls a pot out of the oven, he thumps it. If there's a good ringing sound—if the pot "sings"—it's ready. But if there's just a thud, the pot is put back into the oven. As Max wrote, a person's character is also checked by thumping.[1]

Late-night phone calls, grouchy teachers, grumpy moms, burnt meals, flat tires, you've-got-to-be-kidding deadlines—these are all thumps. Thumps are irritating inconveniences that trigger the worst in us. They catch us off guard and flat-footed. They aren't big enough to be crises, but if you get enough of them, watch out!

Jesus said that out of the nature of the heart a man speaks. There's nothing like a good thump to reveal the nature of a heart. The true character of a person is seen, not in momentary heroics, but in the thump-packed humdrum of day-to-day living.

How do you respond to thumping—to the knocks, blows and trials of life? Do you sing? Or do you thud? Your answer depends to a large degree on what your "pot" is made of—on what's in your heart, as Jesus said.

But even if you have a tendency to thud more than sing, take heart. There is hope. We can learn from the thumps. We can be aware of thump-slump times, such as "blue Mondays" and the return to regular routines after a holiday. No thump is a disaster. All thumps work for good if we are loving and obeying God.

Discuss: What kind of thumps tend to discourage you the most? What are the thump-slump times in your spouse's life? Ask your spouse how you can be sensitive during such times.

Pray: Is your mate or child in a thump slump right now? Pray with him or her that God's grace and love will be real. Then give a wholehearted hug, verbally express your love, and go get an ice-cream cone together.

Note
1. Max Lucado, *Life Lessons: Book of James* (Dallas: Word Publishing, 1996), p. 4.

DAY 27

SETTING
YOURSELF FREE

*If we confess our sins, He is faithful and righteous to forgive
us our sins and to cleanse us from all unrighteousness.*

1 JOHN 1:9

Is your daily life free from the mistakes and sins of the past?
Do you have difficulty letting go of your feelings about people who have hurt you? If so, consider completing a project
we gave a woman a number of years ago.

Mary was bitter. She was angry at her parents for the
neglect she felt as a child and at her husband for his incon-
sistencies. To help Mary begin to put aside her bitterness, we
told her to write a detailed explanation of how her parents
had wronged her and how that had made her feel. She also
listed disappointment after disappointment in her relationship with her husband.

When she finished her list of grievances, she read it
aloud. Seeing her anger on paper and hearing it in her own
words gripped her, and she began to cry.

Through her tears, Mary bowed her head and prayed,
"Forgive me, God. What I've written here is sin. You've

commanded me to honor my parents; I haven't. Instead, I've harbored anger against them for 25 years.

"Forgive me, too," she went on, "for my unloving spirit and critical attitude toward my husband."

When she finished, a great relief swept over her. Mary then took a large red pen and printed across each of the three pages in bold letters the words of 1 John 1:9.

She smiled as she crumpled up those sheets of paper. Then she walked outside, dug a shallow hole and dropped the sheets into it. She lit a match and set the pages on fire. Mary covered the ashes with dirt until the hole was filled, and then she piled seven rocks on top.

Today, when the old bitterness attempts to burst through the soil of her life and she is tempted to look back, she looks at her rock pile. It reminds her that her sins are forgiven and buried.

Discuss: What things from your past need to be buried and forgotten?

Pray: Privately confess any sin to God, and thank Him for cleansing you and forgiving all your iniquities.

MARY COVERED THE
ASHES WITH DIRT UNTIL
THE HOLE WAS FILLED,
AND THEN SHE PILED
SEVEN ROCKS ON TOP.

THE FREEDOM TO FAIL

*Be strong and courageous! Do not tremble or be dismayed,
for the LORD your God is with you wherever you go.*

JOSHUA 1:9

At our house we have experienced plenty of failures, both great and small. For years, a meal without a spill was nothing short of miraculous. The milk may have gone shooting across the supper table or formed a lazy river that cascaded over the edge, splattering onto the floor. We've seen some classic spills: two simultaneously, four at one sitting, and one glass of chilled apple juice that spilled perfectly into Dennis's shoe (while he was wearing it). Our favorite phrase for the children became "It's okay—everybody makes mistakes."

One evening, I spilled my drink during dinner. A little hand patted my arm, and Rebecca (then a five-year-old) reassuringly said, "It's okay, Dad—everybody makes mistakes."

When you give your mate the freedom to fail, you begin to remove the pressure to perform for acceptance. You free your mate to set aside his or her fear—to trust God. Failure then becomes a tutor, not a judge. In the presence of freedom, we learn from failures instead of being condemned by them.

For years, we talked about moving to the country. The thought of the children having room to roam sounded inviting, but moving a large family is a chore. More important, it was a risk. What if we didn't like driving back and forth to town? What if we didn't like being isolated from friends? So we put off the decision.

Then one day Barbara said, "So what if we decide we don't like it? We can sell and move back to town!" Her statement clicked; it gave me the freedom to make a decision—even a wrong one! We decided to try it, and we love it. It's important to note that the freedom to risk making a decision came only after we had given each other the freedom to fail.

Discuss: Share what you would consider to be your greatest failure. How has that impacted your decision-making process today? Discuss a decision you are facing and how the fear of failure is influencing that decision.

Pray: Pray that God will increase your faith to match the challenges you face and that He will teach you how failures have helped you mature in Christ.

WHEN REALITY HITS HOME

*And the seed in the good soil, these are the ones
who have heard the word in an honest and good heart,
and hold it fast, and bear fruit with perseverance.*

LUKE 8:15

*M*any new Christians begin their new lives at an emotional high. They are overwhelmed by God's grace, by the excitement of seeing Him move in their lives and by the love they feel from their new brothers and sisters in Christ. They involve themselves in their churches' ministries and feel the power of God working through them to minister to others.

Then, inevitably, their many glossy-eyed, rose-tinted assumptions about people and life fade when met with massive doses of reality. A trusted Christian friend betrays a brother; a respected church leader commits adultery; people bicker about decisions made by the new pastor. Yes, Christians are full of faults, just like everyone else.

I will never forget Dr. Howard Hendricks's statement one day when I was attending Dallas Theological Seminary. He said, "Gentlemen, if you do not like the smell of sheep, then you'd better get out of the pasture." That statement illustrates the choice you face when reality hits and you realize just how difficult it is to work with people. You can protect yourself by withdrawing from the life of your church, or you can persevere and keep pursuing relationships.

Many Christians today choose the path of self-protection. They move from church to church, never settling down because that would require too much commitment. When you follow this path, however, it's easy to end up cynical and isolated. You miss the joy that comes when you determine not to quit and you allow God to work through you. Then after years of struggling through relationships, you will see the fruit that, as Christ says, only comes through perseverance.

Discuss: When have you been faced with the choice of self-preservation or perseverance? What did you choose?

Pray: Ask God to help you sink roots into a church where you can have years of fruitful ministry.

"LUKE, I DON'T LIKE THAT
RELIGIOUS STUFF, AND
I DON'T WANT TO HEAR
ANYTHING ABOUT IT AGAIN,"
THE WOMAN REPLIED.

LOVE CAN FIND A WAY

*Love is patient, love is kind, and . . . does not take
into account a wrong suffered.*

1 CORINTHIANS 13:4-5

Do you have a family member who resists love or even the Lord? Nina Cameron, who assisted me one year with my sixth-grade Sunday School class, told the class a story I'd like to share with you.

Nina and her daughter met a woman in a nursing home who was known as hard to get along with. Most of the time the woman complained about the nurses, food, room-mates—just about anything she could think of.

"She didn't like anything about us," Nina said, "right down to my name. For some reason she decided to call me Luke." Trying to find some way to reach her, Nina finally asked, "Isn't there anything you like?"

The woman looked up briefly and mumbled, "I like but-terscotch candy and I like to draw." And sure enough, the old woman had quite a talent, although her eyesight was so poor she rarely could finish a drawing.

Nina asked her if she would like her to bring the Bible and read to her. But the woman replied, "Luke, I don't like that religious stuff, and I don't want to hear anything about it again."

Eventually the woman contracted cancer, and Nina could see she was dying. The woman hadn't spoken with her son in years, so Nina called him. Nina breathed a prayer for the Holy Spirit to penetrate through all past pain, and the son finally broke down. "Lady," he said, "I don't know who you are, but I love my mother."

The son didn't have the money to come to see his mother, so Nina purchased a plane ticket. Over the next few days, she had the pleasure of seeing a mother reconcile with her son. And the next time Nina came to the nursing home, the woman had a peaceful look on her face. The woman looked up and said, "Luke, I love you. When you come back, I want you to bring that Bible and read it to me."

Discuss: Do you know someone who resists love? Are there relationships in your life that need to experience healing? What steps have you taken to bring this about?

Pray: Pray that the love of God that penetrates people's hearts will also characterize your own ability to love the unlovable with perseverance.